Faith & Hope

Poems

By

Shirley Ann Wood

Order this book online at www.trafford.com
or email orders@trafford.com

Most Trafford titles are also available at major online book retailers.

Printed in the United States of America.

ISBN: 978-1-4269-6526-5 (sc)
ISBN: 978-1-4269-6527-2 (e)

Trafford rev. 04/09/2011

 www.trafford.com

North America & international
toll-free: 1 888 232 4444 (USA & Canada)
phone: 250 383 6864 ✦ fax: 812 355 4082

FOREWORD

The poems that are included in this manuscript are a collection of writings that I started when I was very young. I became inspired to write these poems by the events that I experienced as I was growing up. I am still writing poems at the age of 82, and will continue as long as I am able.

Over the years I have had great feedback from many readers. This has inspired me to have my poems in print for others to enjoy. I would be more than pleased to know that my poems have inspired or brought comfort to those that will read them.

I have separated my works into two manuscripts one with the title "Heart & Soul" Poems, and the other titled "Faith & Hope" Poems. I have a strong Christian belief and therefore many of my poems, especially the poems included in the Faith & Hope manuscript, will reflect this.

These poems are appropriate for readers of all ages and hopefully will be an inspiration for all that read them.

INDEX FOR "FAITH & HOPE POEMS

THE ANCIENT ONE

"The power" or "The ancient one"
Referred to -- by the scribes --
Views with equanimity -- from somewhere
Deep inside
The universe -- the Earth, when it first began
Pulsating with the pain -- the joy --
Of its all inclusive plan --
Throbbing in its life forms --
With facets -- bright -- divine --
Decreeing all – survive thru love --
Down thru mists of time
In lightning and in thunder
His mighty voice is heard
Yet still as death, this throbbing pulse
At the falling of a bird --
An enigma to the flesh forms -- in his image made
Remolded, by the minds of those decreed by us as "Sage" --
Into a form or concept -- confined by egos great and small --
The wisest may perceive "The Eye"
Shall never grasp -- "The All"
The power -- or -- the ancient one --
Referred to by the scribes

BEHOLD

Behold the Earth – from Heavenly spheres
As it falls from truth and grace
Traveling at light year speed

Thru the dark abyss of space
The lost one, dark his countenance
Guides it deeper still
Into sin, rebellion, by way of Human Will
And high above, a loving God
Takes Pity on our plight
And sends His Son – Our Saviour
The Truth – The Way – The Light
To teach us that we must repent
Of all our evil ways
Help our brother, teach our young
And to our God – Give praise!
Then kneeling humbly He did drink
The final Bitter cup
Suffered All to save us
And once more lift us up
Hard won the grace that we once lost
Paid for on a wooden cross
In agony and torment the saving Blood was shed
A Lamb of God to lift the curse of Death upon our heads
And if we choose we can accept
This precious gift He gave
The gift of everlasting life
Resurrected from the Grave
Hallelujah it is done!
The battle has been fought – And Won
Behold the Earth – from Heavenly spheres
Restored to truth and grace
The gates of Hell could not withstand
God's love for the human Race
So hide no more in darkness
Dwell not in sin and fear
Lift up your hands, your hearts, your mind
Pray – And He will hear!
He'll guide you safely thru this life
And lift you to His throne
For love of Jesus and of you
He'll claim you as His own!

BEYOND THE GRAVE

It seems there is a time – when nothing can be said
Silently by gravesides – we simply bow our heads
We honour all that used to be – thinking it is gone
Mixed with the pain of memory – the haunting strains of song
That once was youth's sweet promise of love forever more
Beguiles the spirit – stays the mind – from closing memories
door
Ah but we must – too bittersweet – to linger way back when!
Lay down the rose upon the grave, leave – begin again
Do not stop to count the cost – the price of dreams once held –
now lost
Know that dreams are gifts from God – no price to high to pay
Thru your sorrow – hope to find – another dream today
For dreams are lovely works of art – painted by the mind and
heart
Of those who love! Believe! And tho it seems
They may be lost – they have been retrieved
For angels gather every one to place in heaven's store
Where lights of hope that brought them forth
Shine forever more
All heaven sees - your pain, your fear
Your loneliness, your heartfelt tears
The courage that it takes to live – in spite of all
To love! To give!
And they shall help you thru
Tho never may they intervene – all choices lie with you
To honour God – with hopes and dreams
To dishonour thru your schemes

It is your life to live – your decision, yours alone
If you shall take - or give!
So if you should decide, to dream a dream once more
Remember – if you stumble – that the very door
That stands at heaven's portals – is a heavy cross
Of one who loved the dreamers – and did not count the cost

CAUGHT IN TIME

I stand upon the border of a strange and unknown land
Memories and mists of time swirl above the strand of Virgin
Beaches,
Running; into infinity of forests dark and brooding -
An undulating sea
Behind me - Devastation - complete and absolute -
Dream cities lie in rubble
Destroyed by bitter truths -
And I ! Have I escaped
The dreadful holocaust?
To walk alone in lands unknown
Until my Soul is lost?
In fear and trepidation,
I hesitate "To Be"
No longer certain I can face
What lies ahead of me
So I stand upon the border
Filled with dreadful fears
Faith and Vision blurring
Thru a veil of burning tears,

4

Why hast Thou forsaken me?
"Once" - My Jesus cried-
As in His pain and agony
To this life - He Died!
So too I - The God is there -
Feed not His Presence - but despair
Tho in truth - I know! -
When the bitter cup is finished
He'll lovingly bestow -
A new life filled with courage
To laugh - To love - To Be!
But in this moment - Caught in
Time - Still - The Agony!

CHRISTMAS SPIRIT

Each Christmas -- as the spirit -- moves upon the earth
And people of each nation --
Celebrate the birth --
Of the gentle Christ Child -- sent by God above,
Our hearts are filled with wonder --
Our souls are filled with love
Many gifts are purchased,
And wrapped with loving care --
We come alive –thru love and joy --
There's magic everywhere
Bells are ringing -- lights are twinkling --
All is gay and bright --
In anticipation of the holy night --

5

When God in all his glory --
Sent the truth -- the way -- the light --
Jesus! Born in Bethlehem in the winter of the land
Redeeming all -- who heed the call
To follow God's commands.

<u>COULD I HAVE LOVED YOU MORE</u>

Could I have loved you more?
I only wish I knew,
Somehow I feel so humble now
Each time I think of you.
Was I too self-centered?
Contrite mean and small?
And were the things that I believed
Important after all?
You gave me life, you gave me love,
Your heart was fine and true
And I was happy, and content
Each time I was with you
But now I often wonder
As I sit alone and yearn
What did I ever do -- or give <u>you</u> in return
God alone can see my heart
And he alone can say
So in my lonely solitude
I can only kneel and pray
I love him, that's the simple truth
I will, always, while I live
Please help me to do more than that
If there's more that I can give
Show me how, guide my heart
In thy holy way
And let me somehow, sometime soon
Feel I can repay
The death of love I feel still rests

Upon this soul of mine
That may become as he was --
Good -- and sweet -- and kind
Without a single thought
That's wrong or smaller mean
But with a mind that's one with God
Pure and fresh and clean
Make me tall in heavens eyes,
Thou I am on my knees,
And I shall cry for happiness
That God has heard my pleas
Help me love for Jesus
Taught " love's the only way"
So let my love in action
become much stronger day by day
Until at last I feel no doubt
No anger and no fear
But walk in perfect certainty
Through all the coming years
For if these things should come to pass
All know and never have to ask
Could I have loved you more?
No -- but I could have told you more,
And even better show you more
But somehow I think that you
Must know, my sorrow and regrets
But note too that the love you gave
I never shall forget
For that is what I hold most dear,
That makes my past so very clear --
Now I must give each day I live
The love you gave to me
To others who might need it
so they too might see
That God gives us to another
That they might teach and guide
Until we grow enough to know
That only love abides.

CRUCIFIED

With preconceived ideas he boldly did defy
With love he healed, forgave, renewed
So they screamed "Crucify!"
Let us slay this gentle one
Set the killer free
Even then he bowed his head in fearful agony
Forgive them Father – help them – for
They know not what they do
Thru my body and my blood
Let them come to you
Since that time the world has pleaded
Send him back again
Praying loudly – to be heard
Above the screams of pain
For while they wait and as they pray
For that great eventful day
They kill all unicorns who stray
Into their great domain
Then kneel and pray to God above
Send back your messanger of love

CRY OF THE HEART

I stand upon the border --
Of a strange, and unknown, land
Where memories and mists of time
Swirl about the Strand -- of Virgin beaches
Stretching -- into infinity

8

Caught in forests dark and brooding
Near an undulating sea
Behind me -- "devastation" --
Complete -- and -- absolute --
Dream cities lie in rubble
Destroyed -- by -- bitter truths!
And I! -- have I escaped the deadly Holocaust?
To walk -- alone -- in lands unknown
Until -- my soul is lost?
In fear -- and trepidation -- I hesitate -- "To BE!"
No longer certain, I can face, what lies ahead of me, --
I stand -- "frozen" on the border --
Of doubt -- and dreadful fears,
Faith and vision blurring --
Through a veil of burning tears.
Why hast thou forsaken me?
"Once" My Savior cried --
As, thru -- His pain and agony --
To this life -- -- he died!
"So too I!" -- Tho God is there!
Feel not -- his presence -- just despair.
Tho -- in truth -- "I know!" --
When this bitter cup is finished
Tis then -- He shall bestow --
A new life! Filled with courage --
"To Laugh" -- "To Love" -- "To Be!"
Lord -- "Give me strength" -- to --
"Hold to you" -- in this my agony.

DAY BY DAY

Day by Day--
My Life is Used--
And Slowly--Slowly--
Dwindles away!
Each morning I awake and thank the Lord
That for my sake--

9

He's given me--
Another day--that all too soon
Becomes the past--"Alas"--
I cannot make it at last,
Like my youth it ages slowly
Till at last--
There'll be no more!
And at the final moment
THE ACCOUNTING!
What did I live for?
What Motive was behind my dreams?
Hopes, desires, efforts, schemes?
I know--within my very soul
By God, who dwells above
That I must base each thing I do
Each thought I think--In Love!
If not in love a deed is done
It is certain I have won
A HOLLOW Victory
No on to care
No God is there
As others of a kind
Shout thru barren earthly halls
The ultimate! Divine!
They worship all that is not true
Counting everything they do
By standards they have set for you
Seem not to know, that day by day
Their life is slipping fast away
They see just what they wish to see
and know just what they know
They are just what they wish to be
And do not wish to grow
They set the rules and keep the peace
And within the human race
Are elevated to a place
Alone--and high above
The one who walks untrodden paths
In the name of Love!

For he who chooses such a path
Must forfeit with his heart
All the glories, men hold dear
And from them now depart
To follow truth, as he has found it in his heart to be!
To share his truth, as he has found it
Thru love--with you--with me!
So do not disregard--the things he has to say
Remember that-- for love of us--the price he had to pay
Know too, he could not pay it
If not for God above,
Who spoke to him--and speaks thru him
In Jesus tender love
Jesus--who became the man
To tell the man of God's great plan
"All Nations bound in Brotherhood!"
Regardless of their race!
For God looks in each human heart
Not at the human face
He cares not what you say you are
Or pertain to be!
He only cares--For love of Him,
How much you care for me!
He only cares about me--as I care for you
He sees our love, or lack of it
In everything we do,

DEAR LORD I LOVE THEM

Thy Son, Oh Lord, so gentle and sweet
Gave Himself to save His sheep
Man, Divine, yea both of these
Thy Holy will He wished to please
So a heavy cross He bore and died on Calvary
And because he died, I dare this night
To beg a boon of Thee
He suffered to save others because He loved them so

The ones I love I need not say
For all of them You know
My innocents, Thy little lambs
So dear to Thee and me
I too would die to save them
If this were asked of me
So keep them safe within Your arms
Protect them all their lives
Let me suffer in their stead
Do not my prayers deny
If any harm is meant for them
I beg You on my knees
Take the cup away from them
And give their pain to me
For gladly would I drink thereof
If they could live and grow
Within Thy Grace – and see Thy face
When it came time for them to go
Back to the heavenly home
From whence they came
To be with Thee, and one another
And if it is Thy Holy Will
To see once more – Their mother
Amen

DESPAIR

Lord I am on my knees
Deep is the Pit, and black as Sorrow
I raise my hands – Lord Please
Ease this pain - this pain
That lasts from yesterday until tomorrow
I can no longer feel so much
I need – I need
Your love, your touch

I need to know someone – somewhere
Can see the devastation that is me
Lift these chains and give me air
Take this life and set me free
Oh my God who gave me life
I've walked so long, so far, alone
End this torment, ease my strife
Lord God <u>*Please*</u> *take me back home*
Lord pity me, I'm on my knees
In pain. My heart Kneels, breaks and Bleeds.
Helpless – I can do no more
But yearn for that far distant shore.

<u>DIVINE PLAN</u>

There lies within the human soul
A light divine and pure
There lives within the human heart
A plan that's true and sure
It was planted long ago
Before our time of birth
A plan bestowed by heaven
To guide us here on earth
And if we listen carefully
To each whispered yes or no
God will tell us every time
The way that we should go
But if we will not listen
Insist we have our say

About the way we choose to go
We soon will lose our way
For if god had His way
And we listened as we should
He'd fill our lives with happiness
For His plan is always good

<u>DWELL WITH US</u>

Sweet Spirit Whisper Softly
To those who listen well
Soft, sweet, words of Wisdom
To drown the screams of Hell
Tell the story once again
About the God who rescued men-
Give them power from above
To crush the hearts of Stone
With Your everlasting love
Restore and bring them home
Soothe away their pain and fears
Gently dry the flowing tears
Make us whole and safe once more
Remove the bitter cup!
From this lost and barren shore
Reach down and lift us up!
Have mercy on the plight of men!
Come! And dwell with us again!

EARTHBOUND

Bound to this Earth
With chains of Mortality
Struggling always
With the forces of Gravity
I long to be Happy like the mirth of a Child
Free like a soft summer breeze
My soul strains upward towards the glory of Heaven
Despair makes me fall on my knees
I view thru tears and an aching heart
The Hatreds – the cruelty of Man
And ponder the reasons that made them depart
From God's Holy – original Plan
I long for the time
When a new world is born
The Banishment of pain and tears
When the light of Heaven
Will fill the Earth
And dissipate all our fears
Until that time I will persevere and do what I must do
But while my body is chained to this Earth
My God! I'm so lonely for You!

THE EXTRA MILE

Lord in my despair--I cried--"What shall I do?"
Your gentle answer--shocked me, for it was--"For who?"
So now that I have pondered--knowing how you care

I offer you this day you've given me
Beginning with a prayer--
Help me use this precious day--hour by hour
In a way--that "you" would have me do
For all that I encounter, I know shall come from you!
It may be the only day that I have left to live--
So guide me thru it as I try--in my small way to give--
Love and hope, truth and light, my service or a smile--
That all may know--that with your aid
"The Robe"--"The Extra Mile"--
That I extended to foe or friend--
Because I love you so
"Is not in vain"
--But helps us all--"In spite of pain"
To grow
So now--Amen--I go your way--see you in awhile
I have a lot that I must do--in "that extra mile".

FAITH

If you care for me at all --
Heed the heartfelt desperate call
That issues to you now
And for me, my only plea -- is --
Your head now bow --
Let your soul reach out for me
Set your imagination free
To seek the rainbow path
Where the unicorns do play --
Where the night turns into day
And gentle wavelet's lap --
Against a wondrous Silver Strand

In a wondrous golden land
With crystal waterfalls --
Where all is well -- as it should be --
And Hell is just a memory --
That holds no fear -- or pain --
While there beseech the powers --
To "Renew" all faith -- again --
For in the tiny mustard seed
Lies a faith so small --
Yet it can move mountains --
If those of faith -- "just call!"
So with your souls -- your love -- your hearts
Ask that all my pain depart --
That I might, my soul, renew!
It cost no worldly "thing" at all
Just -- "The love" -- of -- "You!"

THE FATHER'S DREAM

If one could paint, in words, the Dream-
That lives in eons - yet unseen-
By mortal man, who dwells in sin,
That blights all dreams that live within-
The human heart!
Full of arrogance and pride, We cannot pull the veil aside
With words - or any other means - to describe the wondrous
dream,
Sometimes glimpsed by those who've died-and then returned
For tho they live a span of years-Their soul forever yearns-
To find the words - that would convey - the dream they
glimpsed
That showed the way- "To Life!" Release from pain!
To shed the darkness of the soul - to walk in light again!
Alas they cannot! For they speak - And many will not hear
The simple words cannot defeat, the roaring sound of fear-
The simple truth within their eyes, causes anger to arise
In pride they scream - Be still! Defensive now-

They mock the dream - Knowing their free will-
Is theirs to keep - to do with - whatever they would choose
Who are _you_ to tell them "By their will" -they win _or_ lose?
For Will is just a word for "Choice" we choose what we shall
be
God's will is that we share his dream- It's left to you and me-
To choose the path His Son once walked-
The Truth! The light! The way!
Or stumble in the darkness of lies, where souls decay-
Lost forever - they shall dwell
In the fallen angel's hell-
Wherein the soul does scream
If only I could trade my will- for love

FOR THE LOVE OF GOD

I have asked my God, _Your_ God,
To help me to impart
To the Jewish nation the love within my heart
The gratitude I feel for you
The chosen ones of the yore
The gentle nation picked by God
To open up the door-
So others of the world could see
The Glory of Eternity.
For among you there was born
On one dark cold night
A baby who was destined
To become a light-
Within the minds - the hearts and souls
Of peoples far and wide
Banishing all pagan fears
That we keep locked inside
For he told us, as no other had
Of your God above-
His Wisdom – Power - Glory
And his universal love

He exorcised the demons
That would lead us into hell
Showed us how simple faith and love,
Could restore, and make us well
Where there was death, he gave us life
When on Calvary, he hung
Upon a cross for us
In dreadful agony
No wonder I adore him-
I would think that you would too
Consider how he changed the world
This simple, wondrous Jew
Gods's only Begotten Son
He was the purest, and the greatest one in loving
Truly in obedience
The Saviour of the rest of us,
Who in his truths abide
A haven for the weary - who in his love reside.
Yes he was Jewish, and not a
Christian - But his life you see
Altered our way of thinking
So" Christianity"-
Became the greatest of all God's gifts
Forgiveness for you and me

FORGIVE ME

I would weave colours, clear and fine
With this single life of mine
In the tapestry of time!
Or paint with multicoloured hue
Each single thing I say or do
With brilliant shades – pure and true!
"I would be" – As music, music of the spheres
Vibrant and exciting – mellowing with years
Into a soft sweet melody –
Ah! I would be! I would be!

So tell me God – how came I here?
To this discordant vale of tears – where gentle souls must
yearn?
Where the whiplash of humanity – in callous unconcern
Marks – with strife – with torment - those who follow Thee
Screaming – "Crucify the King – set Barrabbas free!"
And freely does Barrabbas roam – his fruits are everywhere!
Growing from the seeds we plant – of fear – of hate – despair!
And those, who dawn thru eons, since the very dawn of time
Born of love, formed in hope, in Thy eternal mind
Who would - personify thru faith – all You'd have them be
Fail! Or falter! In this world of such iniquity
Look not upon – what they've become
But what – they longed to be
Remember not their failures
But – their love of Thee
I ask – for I am one who
Thru your Son Devine
Dares to Beg forgiveness
For this wasted life of mine!
Amen

THE GIFT

There is a place beyond this mortal strand,
A bright and pure and holy place, a fine eternal land
Who dwells within? What sort of wondrous people can these be?
Why don't you know? Just simple folk the same as you and me,
In each of us within this life a bit of glory lives
To each of us a special gift the God of glory gives
Perhaps the gift is laughter that we may make others smile
Or a gentle understanding that for a little while --
We may share with someone who is saddened, heavy burdened,
or in pain

But what ere the gift God gives us no two are quite the same
So many gifts so varied, strength, wisdom, hope and love --
And every time we use them he watches from above
And when at last we stand before him in that great eternal land --
The human errors we have made he'll fully understand
He'll know of our temptations the secret thoughts we tried to hide
He'll know the burdens that we carried
The greed, the hate, the pride,
And then He'll look within the hearts of loved ones left behind,
And there He'll find the best of us the only glory of mankind
Our love for one another our compassion and our tears
The good things taught to others the work of many years
The times we tried so very hard

To do all we could do

To give each other hope and faith

And gratitude for you

Amen

GIVE ME

Give me a soul that's filled with peace
Give my troubled mind release
Free me of these bonds of fear
Let me feel that you are near
Take my hand and walk with me

Fill my heart with love for thee
Dispel the darkness, grant me light
That I may always do what's right
Keep my loved ones in thy grace
That they and I might see thy face,
From all evil keep us free
That someday we me dwell with thee
One thing more of thee I pray --
Accept my thanks for thy gifts today.

GOD IS THERE

I entered church suitably dressed
And sedately walked down the aisle
Nodded briefly to many friends
Not one of whom would smile
They all sat in their Sunday dress
With faces set and stern
Sometimes glancing sideways
Or grasping a child who tried to turn
I heard the Padre read the text
Knowing his sermon was coming next
Heard little of what he had to say
For the coughing and scuffling of feet
He looked very tired, spoke low that day
And I became dizzy with the heat
I left the church, felt I would cry
But as I walked neath the clear blue sky
And the sunlight made streamers thru the trees
And I felt on my cheek a clean sweet breeze
A brook running crystal clear o'er its bed
Kept time to the hymn that still rang in my head
And suddenly God was very near
And I knew why Jesus walked neath the sky

And preached on a hilltop bare
Why He'd loved the sea
And all natural beauty
For surely God was there
With people who worked 'til the sweat poured down
Children or guppies, harlots and clowns
With doctors and wise men, musicians and wives
With everyone, everywhere all of their lives
But open the doors of your temples wide
Or you'll not find Jesus there inside
He'll be instead with someone you scorned
Because His heart was simple and warm.

GOD IS LOVE

"God is love - All else is vanity"

I am the way, the truth, and the light,
These things my sweet Saviour said --
So my children I ask but one thing from thee,
When the day comes -- This world says I'm dead --
I ask for _one_ prayer -- to help me -- to help you
Altho there are many -- just this one will do --
"Show us the way, the truth and the light
Stay with us now -- for grief is like night"
Tho sometimes it seems it never will end
If embraced it will prove not a foe but a friend
For in it we rest, remember, and dream,
Until the bright light of day
And there _will_ come a time sweet Love's of mine
When our anguish will all melt away
Just follow" His Way-" "Love" each other --

Then the" Truth" of forgiveness you'll see
And the" Light" from above --
Through your truth and your love
Will bless all and set your spirits free!

THE GREATEST OF THESE

All those I love – who – love return
I hold – within my heart!
Thru love alone – eternally
They become a part
Of all the best! That there can be
In heaven – or – on earth
Thru – love alone – their loyalty
Bespeaks – a Godly worth
That lets me know – as they reach out
With healing – heart and hand
The gentle spirit dwelling there -
Who always understands
The depths of my confusion
The depths of my despair
In my night – my fearful fright
Always – they are there!
Their tears of sweet compassion
Their words of hope to me
Break – the chains – that cause me pain
For they – would have me – free!
The rainbow children – sent by God
The promise – from above

Touching earth – touching hearts
With beauty and with love
From God – they come – so God I praise
That such as these – Exist!
Treasures! – stored within my heart
Sealed with a grateful kiss!

GROUND ZERO

I love you - I have - always
But I don't know what to do-
You've given me so many gifts-
But all I want-
Is you!
You burden me so very much
Yet you withhold your tender touch
It seems I'll never be
For you don't tell me - ever!
What you want of me.
But others have and others do!
All telling me-
For love of you - I must give and give
For them - for life - for love of you-
Give all – and - cease to live.
I've given all - I have to give
In life - In love - I've ceased to live
There's nothing left for me-
I gave it all for love of you-
So I have ceased to be-

There is you - And those you love
- And me- Whoever -and Whatever -
In Hell - or Heaven - Be!

GUIDANCE PRAYER

Lord -- I'm very tired
Don't know what to do
Have no idea where to turn
So Lord I turn to you
I know that you will listen
For I know you truly care
Even when my soul deplores
That you are even there
For something's happened to me Lord
I somehow can't explain
I lost your lovely gift of faith
In my abyss of pain
Can't find it any more Lord
Hurts too much to try
Tho the loss is agony
I cannot even cry
Lord I can hardly feel at all
What has gone wrong with me?
Why must I live in shackles
When I long so to be free?
But if I must abide such pain
Never find my faith again
In Jesus name I ask

Give me the strength that I will need
To complete my tasks
Then thru his blood -- thru his love
Forgive me Lord I pray --
Take me home -- to be with you and bid me Lord to stay --

THE HARVEST

The rainbow path leads upward
"Beyond" -- man's comprehension --
To beauty, spirits filled with love --
Unknown in our dimension
Once -- long ago -- the human race --
Descended from this wondrous place --
Wherein our God doth dwell --
Spilled brother's blood upon the earth --
To feed the tares of hell --
Since then they've grown -- side by side --
The tares among the wheat --
One fed by blood -- One saved by blood
The circle -- incomplete!
On the cross -- our Lord did know
That tho he died for <u>all</u>
Those there were, who, like the tares
Would never heed his call --
Those who <u>do</u> -- for love -- <u>Returned</u> --
In humble expectation -- <u>Bow their heads</u> --
For great the weight --

Of coming to fruition
But <u>soon</u> -- the harvest shall begin --
As he gathers up "His own" --
And leads them on his rainbow path --
Back to their ancient "Home"!

<u>HE</u>

"He" created all – beyond – what we know or see
Such wonders He created in such complexity
That there's no creature – anywhere – in all the universe
That can hope to understand the beauty and the worth
Of all that "The Creator" in the beginning, had in mind
For us created in His image – and called by Him – mankind
In love He fashioned all of us –
And each and every one He calls by name and knows us
Each daughter and each son
Yet knowing this we often walk - with head bowed in despair
Bending wills instead of hearts – forgetting He is there
We live in bondage to the earth and cannot be set free
Until – Unless – we once more know
All we are! Can be!
Thru the power of creation He calls us to employ
The gifts of faith, of light, of hope
To build and not destroy
So seek His truth – obey His word – and very soon you'll find
Peace beyond all understanding
Of heart and soul and mind
For He can then restore you!
As He wipes away the tears
Lovingly He'll hold you close
Dispelling all your fears
For He, your Father – loves you!
No matter what you be!
But for you - to know this! He asks –
Please turn to Me!

For He cannot help you ever – unless you wish it so
Your own free will gives you the choice
Of which way you shall go
So just remember – every day – you choose your destiny!
To live in bondage to the world –or
Thru Christ – Be set free
It you choose the latter
He'll reveal to you – your worth
Bless each effort made thru Him
And give you love, and peace, on earth

HELP ME LORD

Help me Lord to write a poem --
Not that I may hence be known
As a mortal great in deed
But as your child who's sown a seed
A seed bestowed from heaven above
Containing in its heart -- Your love
The essence of the greatest souls
Of whom all wondrous tales are told
The essence of the very earth
Of each new miracle of birth
Give me the insight to impart
To those who are of heavy heart
Because they fail to see --
That often they have given birth
Tho they have not prodigy --
If they took another's hand to
Comfort them in loss --
Or gave them courage to go on
No matter what the cost
If they made another laugh
When they wanted just to cry
If they made them want to live
When they wanted just to die
If they took away their fear

Touched their hearts, dried their tears,
Stood by them on a fateful day,
Knelt with them as a bent to pray,
They have bestowed their gifts of worth
And thru these gifts -- have given birth
To faith, to hope, to love --
The essence of the greatest souls
Blessed by God above --
I know! For I've received them
When I was troubled so --
And to each of you who gave to me
I'd like you all to know --
I could not have lived without your help --
In the heartfelt way I do --
And hope with all my heart and soul
I've given back to you,
A fraction of your wondrous gifts
That's made my life so full -- so rich
I owe so much -- and small indeed --
Is the tiny little seed -- by which
I'm sometimes known --
My ability to write -- impart --
And sometime touch another's heart
With some prose or poem --
I only wish that I could write the words
The better to impart –
How precious is each tiny seed --
If love is at its heart --
The world has need of each of them
A harvest for the earth --
To feed the hungry -- heal the sick,
And finally, give birth --
To a bright new era -- where we walk hand
In hand – and find once more
What once we lost – Love's golden
Promised land.

HOPE

There is a place where hope doth dwell
A long way--from the bowels of Hell
A long way from deceit and schemes
In loving eyes--and living dreams
In hands extended in time of need,
In words of faith--in faith indeed--
In someone standing firm and true
In one who has a faith in you--
In one who never lets you down
Or places on your head a crown--
Of thorns to wound your mind
Who does not make you bear a cross
For others of mankind
Hope, that will not wound you
With sword straight to the heart,
Abiding there without despair
When others all depart
Faith, that when all hope seems dead
They'll gently carry you instead
Until you rise again knowing that thru love,
the narrow Law of Men--
Can be overcome, by the miracle called hope--
But to most who don't believe--narrow is it's scope
They see it as impossible,
So loudly they do cry,
There's no way a camel could pass through a needle's eye,
There's no resurrection once a hope is dead,
So they see the Cross--the end!
When they should see--instead--
The glory of a hope fulfilled,
Thru sacrifice and love,
The gift bestowed on caring hearts
By God who dwells above,
Surpassing understanding of the multitude who scorn,
Known only to the ones who hope--
The ones who are Reborn!

HOPE

The Torture's "over" - Now - They say -
So do not dwell on yesterday -
Be Grateful you - survived!
Try to forget - and do not dwell -
On Glimpses of your Private Hell -
Be Glad, to be Alive!
They are right! - Life must go on -
and tho the days and nights be long,
They Finally - do End!
And there is, hope, and comfort -
Each time you find a friend -
Who reaches out - Who touches you -
Who seems - somehow - to know -
That tho you have survived the pain -
And thru it - - Learned to grow!
That Sometimes, you're still fearful -
And the World derides -
You cannot stop the tears that flow -
So you recede - And Hide -
Until the Wave of memory - That caught you unaware
Be once more battled - overcome - By Courage and by Prayer
Tis then - Alone - Except for God - One surely would be Lost,
But Thru His Sacrifice - and Love - He justifies the cost
"Of Believing!" Once again! For He - Believes in Me!
And Has Promised - Thru His Son - To Set all Sinners Free-
So I hold unto His Word - With knowledge it is True -
Praise Him for each new Blessing - And Thank Him "friend"
for you!

HUMILITY

I am ashamed of all I am. Why aren't you and you?
I am less than any man. I know this to be true.
If I am proud it is because God loves my poor intent
And because He loved me to this world He sent
A Mortal yet immortal Soul who paid the price for me
Jesus his beloved Son Sent to Set me free.

I ALONE

To Hurt - To Blame - Was Not My Aim -
When, In My Deep Despair -
I Reached For Help, And Understanding -
And Found - "You Didn't Care!"
From This Pit Of Quicksand - I Called Out
"Please Throw A Rope"-
And You Replied - "Within Yourself Is Your Only Hope"
There Was A Time When You Were Here,
In This Hellish Place!
Twas Then You Pleaded - "Help Me!"
"Thru You, I Find God's Grace!"
How Quickly You've Forgotten, The Needs Within Us All -
How I Threw You The Rope Of Love - In Answer To Your Call
Drew You From The Quicksand Of Your Deep Despair,
Does God, Not Work Thru You As Well?
So Why Are You - Not There?
You Cannot Seem, To Understand-
He Wears A Human Face,

Love, Is His Only Channel, In The Human Race
If We, Do Not Acknowledge This -
Like Judas - With Betraying Kiss -
We Give To Calvary - A Victim Of God's Love Denied
A Person To Be Crucified - Is This Your Wish For Me?
Remembering For Love Of You, The Day That Jesus Died -
You Seem To Have Forgotten - "Two Thieves Were Crucified"
He Cared!
Yes - Just Because Of This! The Other?
Went The Judas Way - Bestower Of The Kiss -
That Had No Love Or Meaning - Except To Prove The "I"
"I" "Alone" Does Not Condone -
It Always Crucifies!

IF NOT FOR YOU

Because of you we've come to know
The one true Living God
The Greatest Gift to Mankind
That broke the Iron Rod
Formed into yokes and weapons
To Keep Man In Slavery
Because of you, in Bondage
We struggled to be free!
Aspiring to greater heights
We lit our lamps to Quell the night
And Hailed The Father On His Throne
Throughout the world to make it known
The message that you shared with us
In God and Freedom we must trust!
Because of you our world began
And lifted spirits high
From the realm of pagan man
To realms beyond the sky

If not for you
We would not know the Father of the Son
How could Christianity
Ever have begun?
We truly love our Saviour
And are grateful for his birth,
His sacrifice for love of us,
Is treasured here on Earth
The Chosen one--The Son of God
Born of the Chosen Race
Who spread the news throughout the world
Of the Father's Saving Grace
Ah yes I know we differ
In some theology
But with the same God given right
To keep our spirits free
But we would not have the knowledge
If it hadn't been for you
Courageous Sons of Abraham
The freedom loving Jew

JESUS

Many words are written of Who and what you are
Of your birth, your life, your death, of the Brilliant Star
That guided wise men, Humbled Shepherds In that long ago
And they proclaimed your holy name so all the World would
know,
Your were the Saviour sent to Earth to teach, to heal, to save,
That we, through you, could rise above the Status of a slave,
Ah! That I could only show by what I say and do -
The glory that I feel inside, each time I think of you,
If I were gifted I could paint a portrait so divine,
That all would clasp the image fast until the end of time
Or if I were a poet - I could touch the heart

35

Of those who have not known you - then they'd become a part -
Of You - and all you stand for, And there-by learn to live
In such a way - that day by day - their very best they'd give!
But I cannot, for you see - within this world, the least is me.
So I shall simply Honour you - In my own small way
And thank Our Father for your love - your guidance day by day.

THE JOURNEY

To tell of her great journey -- in another land --
The love she had encountered, the beauty of the man
But words somehow could not convey the wonders in her mind --
And then she found to her dismay, that others of her kind,
Found her damaged! different now!
No longer bright and quick and smart --
In her pain -- she called again -- to the one within her heart --
He lifted her, each time she wearied, down thru the many years,
He counseled her through many doubts, and gently dried her tears
He helped her understand the ones -- full of mockery --
Saying – it's not what you have said,- it's your love for me --
That makes them turn upon you -- these dwellers of the night
It angers them to be revealed in my holy light
Some of them, at one time walked, a better way you see
Perhaps some day they shall again
Choose light, and truth through Me

JUST CALL

When I was a child,
Sometimes at night –
My dreams were bad,
And so with fright –
I'd awake and call
Turn on the light1
I'm afraid of the dark
I cannot see-
Something evil – is after me
Twas then that my mom or dad would hear
Come into my room and hold me near
They'd rock me gently in their arms
Protecting me from imagined harm
Saying – shhhh, there is nothing to fear

Safe within their arms - once more –
I'd gently drift to Elysian shores
Waking to the morning light
Where suddenly my world was bright
Then I would laugh at all my fears
For I was safe, if they were near.

As I grew older I forgot
These lessons I had learned
And in the terrors of my nights
For love and peace I yearned
Until the night that was so dark
That terror gripped my soul
I could not move to find the light
There was no place to go
No one to hear or answer me
Death seemed so near, a certainty.
Twas then God heard and came to me
He said I love you, never fear –
When all are gone – I am here
I never shall abandon you
Just place your trust in Me

Rest now in My arms this night
Till in My light you see
Had you not been so afraid
You'd have no need of Me
And if you had not needed Me
Though I would have loved you still
You would not know how much I love you
And that My holy will
Has power to release you
From all – or any plight
To make you happy through your day
To comfort you at night
Just trust Me, and believe in Me
That all things work for good
For those who love Me shall be blessed
And if you ever should
Be assailed with fear or doubt
Know that I am near
Just call for Me in Jesus' name
And I shall always hear
My angels will all serve you
And my children of the earth
Will comfort and uphold you
For your faith shall make your worth
More than that of purest gold
For each child of Mine you see
Shall walk in love, and praise, and joy
For all eternity!

THE KINGDOM

Beautiful Holy Spirit, caught in the wee ones' smiles
Bestowing her strength on the travelers of life, over the weary
miles
She cradles the heads of the dying – kisses their fevered brow
Quells all their fears – drying their tears with love – forever

theirs now!

Delicate! Strong! An enigma is she – touching all souls who
long to be free
With the power of heaven – the Trinity – One – grace of the
Father – Spirit and Son
Bonded in love – we can't understand – yet the spirit of love –
sweeps 'cross the land
Holding the chalice – full to the brim – with the
Blood that was shed to save us from sin
Sent by the Saviour – she left the great throne
Commanded be God – "Mark with love – all our own!"
Praise her now, and the powers that sent her
To be with us yet – for awhile
See her truth and her love and her beauty
Caught up in the wee ones' smiles
("Of such as these – is the Kingdom of Heaven made!"

LETTER TO JESUS

Dear Jesus your love is so sweet
It enfolds me and life is complete
I came to the cross, bewildered and lost
And laid all I was at your feet
You looked with compassion and love
Held me up to the Father above
Said – behold she is mine
In our nature divine she is cleansed
And restored in our love
Then the spirit descended on me

Broke the chains that I might be free
Now the Lord dwells within
I am filled to the brim
And the glory of God now I see
I would praise you Dear Jesus so sweet
And lay all my love at your feet
Your pain is my pain, again and again
Just want to repent and repent
Jesus – the sweet name of love
Father dear Father above
Spirit Divine – All are now mine
And I soar like a newly freed dove
Praise You – Glory to You
I am free – I am loved – I am new
My soul swells with pride – To be newborn – alive
Alive dear sweet Jesus in you!

LEGACY

I love you because of many things
Too numerous to state
But mainly because of your gifts of love
And your total lack of hate
Your love makes each day better
For me, and all those you meet -
When others are tough and the world is rough
Your love is a safe retreat
I think of you, your gentle touch,
The compassion you so readily share
And even tho you are far away -
It's as if, in my need, you are there!
Then my heart fills with gratitude

For your undying love
My eyes fill with tears, as I thank God above
That He loved me enough, to send you to me,
That He Behold, and decided, this was all meant to be
"By their Fruits you shall know them" He clearly states,
Where God's Love abides, there's no room for Hate
By your Fruits I have known you, down thru the years
Thru good times, and bad times, Laughter, and tears
Always you're Stalwart, gentle and brave,
Such as you are, tho it goes to the Grave,
Cannot live there, so rises, On wings of pure Love,
To it's place in God's House of Treasures above
This He has stated - which makes it so,
On Earth or in Heaven it shall flourish and grow
For Love is of God, His Essence, His seed,
Use it wisely but well, for both worlds have a need,
For the Beauty it brings to each Hungry soul
And the hope that it Brings to Mankind as a whole
If you don't believe in these things I have said
And to you - when you die, all you are is now dead
That's not true, for all the things that you taught,
Shall live on in others - shall not die and rot
Like the Shell that you wore while on Planet Earth
But go on thru the decades, be they Vile or of worth.

LIFE'S ROAD

Sometimes – very seldom
As you travel down life's road
You'll find someone – who sometimes
Will share your heavy load.
But you'll never tell by looking
Just who that one will be
For some you think are kind and good
Are full of treachery.

41

And some you never cared for
Never tried their love to win
May be the very person
Who's the good Samaritan
Could be a he – could be a she
Could be young or old
You'll never tell by looking
Who's heart is warm or cold
But when you're sad and weary
And you're sure that no one cares
That's the time – Thru grace of God
That someone will be there
And when they clasp your hand
And your faith in life renew
Remember to repay the debt
When someone's needing you.
For every deed of kindness
Every act of love
Is cherished by the Angels
In that treasure house above.

LISTEN

Listen to my heart --It weeps within my soul --
Impart your wisdom-- your love and warmth -- for I am very
cold
So cleanse me Lord and robe me --
In linens white and fine
Place upon my brow -- the mark that I am thine.

Tho my body is in bondage, set my Spirit free --
So when there is no more to do --
No more you'll ask of me --
I may leave this vale of tears
Place my gift of many years -- lived for you alone --
Among the others offered at the base of your great throne

LOVE OF JESUS

I hear a whisper – I love you
In this love abide
I am the way – the truth – the light
Do not your talents hide
Believe a little longer
And I shall set you free
For when you hold yourself so high
You reach in love to Me!
I know it isn't easy
To hold to things unseen
That sometimes – God – the best of you
Is looked on like a dream
But tho you're mocked – and tho you're hurt
And even when you doubt
Wondering why you were born
What life is all about
I see your vast complexities
Your burden to be you
Brought about for love of me
While trying to be true

To your own self - "Within the World!"
A Herculean task
To prevail – thru travails
I know – and yet I ask!
For as I am the best of you
If in the trying you stay true
You are the best of me.

THE MASTER'S HAND

To see you happy -- Ah what a joy t'would be --
To hear your laughter echoing my dreams for you
Would make my life worth while that, and all that
I've believed in -- live in eternity!
Eternity -- the wondrous word -- spoken of in poetry
Glimpsed in paintings done by a master's hand
The destiny of all who know -- deep within their very soul
There is a master's plan!
But who is left to listen, to the whisper in the din?
So much to see, to want, to have, beckoning to draw you out --
How many look within?
And when they do -- a tiny peek -- to see if all goes well,
Then reassured they turn their backs,
Shrug their shoulders, join the pack -- and run
Like lemmings to their own peculiar hell.
But there are some who linger thru an instinct to survive,
They don't keep pace, and when the race, destroys itself
A few are left alive!
And so the wheel begins to turn -- each nation in its time,

Struggles -- grows and reigns supreme --
Loses all the wondrous dreams --
That made it strong and fine,
And with it go the young the old,
The rebels brave, thy leaders bold
And drifting in the meadows in seeming revelry,
Are all that's left -- the dreams!
How happy they would be --
To hear their children's laughter, the gift they long to give --
Love, and hope, and happiness as long as they should live.
The only worthwhile thing on earth
The first -- the Masters plan, designed to bring the peace we
seek by the Masters hand!

MY GOD

Do you hear me?
Is your spirit here in the silent, dark of night?
Even the Wise Men waited
And watched for Your heavenly beacon light
And it shone
Bright and certain
And from the three corners of the earth
It guided them by night and day
To the place of Jesus' birth
I too am searching for an answer
To quell my restless soul
But I need your beacon light
To guide me to my goal

I've searched <u>my soul</u> – <u>my heart</u>, <u>my mind</u>
For the thing You'd have me do
Now I am weary with the searching
And appeal <u>again</u> to You!
You're my Father
You love me
Help me!
This is my simple prayer
Send me a dream in the dark of night
Lead me from darkness into the light
Send <u>me</u> a Heavenly Beacon Light!
Help me!
God help me!

<u>MY LIFE - YOUR LIFE</u>

When I was young my heart did dare to hope
In shy and timid words, in hesitating gentle ways it spoke
In awe and wonder it beheld the wisdom of the older folk,
And tried to emulate, to please, to fulfill their dreams for me,
Their plans, as in persuasive tones they'd coax --
Each one seemed to me so wise, but something lost
And hidden deep within their eyes
Made me uneasy -- but then I'd think, 'tis just my youth,
That makes me doubt as at my fears they'd wink
And so I listened, learned, and followed each of my mentors in their turn,
And quelled the tumult deep within, thinking it was wrong,
Would lead to sin – to yearn,
For forbidden paths, that always beckoned me,
And whispered so persistently
Of other spheres, where those who dared to venture were
In some way - so completely free

46

I could not understand how, facing unknown perils,
In strange uncharted places this could be,
So once again I listened to the older wiser ones
Who said they knew, of all that troubled me,
But that I must resist for the voice was no account
And my dear with ought us here you simply will amount -- to
nothing!
Now fear was my companion for within the human race,
To be as nothing, is to not exist, to matter,
Or even have a place
A situation to be avoided no matter what the cost
And so I crucified each desire in its turn until they <u>all</u> were lost
And took my place as years went by among the older folk,
Guiding and deciding until one day a young and shy and timid
girl,
In hesitant uncertain words turned to me and spoke --
Of some small voice that told her of <u>all</u> that she could be,
And in some way had discerned that once, perhaps,
Such a guide had dwelt within the soul of <u>me</u>,
Twas then a cry of anguish rose from deep within my very soul
A cry that shattered time and space and saw as thru a corridor
--
Another girl, another face
Full of hope, ability <u>unique</u> to her thru grace
<u>My God</u> -- <u>The voice</u> – '<u>twas you</u> -- is <u>you</u> -- the one that I
denied
Rejecting you -- your wondrous gifts -- following the cheering
crowd
As your life, my life
"I Crucified!"

<u>NIGHT</u>

In the stillness of night
My mind rides wings of fancy and of fact
Darting, seeking, soaring, into

The future or the past
Like some frantic creature
Always searching
Forward here and back
Dissecting moments looking
For a spark of truth or love
Pondering the death of sea
The vastness of the earth
The mysteries of unknown
Galaxies alone
Wondering why, what was, now
Has ceased to be
Longing to understand all
Things especially my God!
What am I to him and more
What is he to me?
Do I really love him? Do
I sincerely believe
What sort of spirit is he? Does
He laugh and does he grieve?
Or is he impassive distant?
Like the stars that shine at night
I guess I'll never ever know
Four with the morning light comes
Mundane things that must be done
So I try to do what's right
Knowing later -- when all the
Worlds asleep my mind once
More will soar and seek

<u>NOT MINE TO GIVE</u>

The gift I'd like to give you
It's just not mine to give --
The wondrous gift of happiness
As long as you should live
A life as rich as heaven --
With laughter hope and love.
And every blessing possible
Showered from above --
But since I cannot give this gift
I'll simply kneel and pray --
That God shall grant you all these things
On this Christmas day

<u>ONCE AGAIN</u>

Come to me God -- come to me <u>now</u> --
For I can no longer wait
Lay your cool hand on my fevered brow --
For the hour of my life's growing late
Sing me your song -- the song of the spheres
Wipe out the pain -- wipe out the tears --
Take me back to be once more with thee,
Let all that I am, and all that I was
Be ended as you set me free --
Come to me God, come to me now
For I'm weary of all life contains
I want to go back to your heart and your love,

To find comfort -- and me --
"Once again"

THE PLAN

Oh my God! I do not doubt --
That <u>you</u> know what <u>you're</u> about!
That you have a special plan --
For each woman and each man --
I've always held this to be true --
Tho I don't know what to do!
For the question is -- you see!
What do you expect of me?
Am I right? <u>or</u> Am I wrong?
Am I weak? <u>or</u> Am I strong?
I don't know – for tho I pray --
I felt <u>so</u> <u>alone</u> today!
I need your strength to aid and guide --
Your wisdom when I must decide --
Your gift of faith -- to know -- believe --
Your patience when I've been deceived --
To forgive and understand --
Your loving, healing, gentle hands --
To give a meaning once again --
To not give up, to not give in --
For I have walked the desert now --
So very long -- it seems --
That all I thirst and hunger for –
Is you and rest and dreams

THE PHONE CALL

I spoke to my daughter on the phone today
And everything I had to say
Well I'm afraid it wasn't good
For things weren't going as they should
There were no answers I could find
That would give me peace of mind
I spoke of how very hard I'd tried
And then just plain broke down and cried
Then a little voice so sweet and mild
Came thru from my beloved child
Mom you try too hard – I find
Don't you know that God is blind?
You see when he accepted you
Thru His beloved Son
All your sins were washed away
Every single one
Your hair's not brown, your clothes don't count
You're eyes aren't grey or blue
He only sees the soul inside
And not the mortal you
His love and glory blinds Him
To what you are in others' sight
He only sees that lovely little, singing, dancing light
That lives inside – your spirit!
So in your spirit worship Him
And He will bless and guard you
From all the pains of sin
I sat and held the telephone
And praised God's holy name
Thru my daughter's loving heart
His love He did proclaim
For suddenly within me
Was a great unfolding light
That let me know how blind He is
Yet precious in His sight
Of all the times I've told my daughter this
She's kept my words within her heart

And returned them like a benedictory kiss
Like bread upon the waters – returning to the shore
No matter what the burdens – I am God's once more!

<u>*PLEASE LORD*</u>

What has happened to my Life?
Lord, I need to know
All the things I hoped for
Well--they just aren't so!
What happened? When?
And why? is everything perverse?
Seems so bitter! Meant to be?
All things in reverse?
Lord you know I trust you
To know what's best for me!
I only ask with all my heart
That you will help me see
If it's your will, these things are so
To help me understand and grow,
At this time I feel uncertain
Lonely and alone
I have no strength or courage
To face things on my own
Alone I am a vessel
Broken with despair
Crying Lord please help me
Let me know that you are there!
If I can feel your presence
My courage will renew,

For Lord all things are possible
With you--
But just--
With you!

MY PRAYER !

Dear Lord –
I know You're busy
With so much you must do,
But I want to send a message
And it has to go thru You!
Tell my Dad I love him
Much more than I can say
Tell him that I miss him
And think of him each day
Tell him all the good things
Just forget the bad
You see he loves me
Very much and that would
Make him sad
Oh yes – of course I do not know
Just when You'll want me to go
But please tell him
When it will be
Because dear Lord
He'll want to be
On hand to smile
And welcome me

THE PRAYER

I'd like to pray – and right away
Hear Your voice in fact
A yes or no – but definite
So I'd know how to act
They say a tiny voice is somewhere deep inside
But listen tho I do my Lord
It seems mine runs and hides
At least I never hear it
I'm never ever sure
Which way to go or what to do
What is right or wrong
I want to know which way to go
But sort of drift along
And so I seem to have no purpose
Tho I'd like one very much
So if You cannot speak to me
Then let me feel Your touch
Push me if You must, in any way You choose
But send me somewhere dear Lord God
Before my life I lose!
For when my life is finished
And death has dealt the final Blow
I'd like to offer <u>something</u>
Some talent God to show
For all the years I've lived
You see – I can't stand waste
And I'd like to stand before you proudly
When we meet face to face.

PRIORITY

'Tis a day for Pondering - the gray Mists
Hang heavy in the trees.
Burdening their branches - Bending them low,
No sun - no breeze
To relieve the terrible oppression.
It is as if the wooded Glen,
Reflects the spirit of Burdened Men
Who cannot lift their heads or hearts
Because of dull routine.
Rooted to the spot, they cannot wander.
Know not the vastness of the world,
Have no goal - no dream.
Ah poor creatures - you do not delight the soul or eye.
Give no shelter, leave cold each heart of those who pass you
by.
What purpose Serve Ye?
There are other places - other people
Where warmth and love abound.
The Gypsy - in his wisdom wanders always
Following the paths of Sunlight
Where laughter can be found.
Children of God _delight_ in life and fill each shining hour,
With laughter - compassion, faith and Hope.
Their life like a tall White Tower
Stands High
For everyone to see — Reflecting the Builder who
Block on block reached towards Eternity.
For the Tower is filled with those whose life the builder
touched.
For some he did only a little.
For others He did much!
The knowing heart looks deep inside
Sees the desperation there
Does not turn to run and hide
But takes the time to care.
As _He_ cares — so he is cared for, and when
His time is done - He leaves a legacy.

For those he loved – in turn will love – someone.
And tho his name may be forgotten
By the sons of Man
The Angels sing a wondrous song
Of how it all began – And his NAME is sung in Celestial Halls
for all Eternity.
And the Hope of Heaven
The fate of Earth – is "Bequeathed"
TO YOU
TO ME!

THE RED MANTLE
"Armistice Day"

Behold the red mantle

As it softly waves

In the distance it appears soft and warm

A cloak we are told to protect all that are cold, hungry,

despairing, forlorn.

As they reach out to grasp at its hem never noticing over their

heads

That the mantle has deepened to the colour of black as it

undulates lowers and spreads

Then slowly and softly it folds round its prey

These unwitting victims of fate

And beneath the red mantle their pitiful cries "There's no air,

we suffocate"

And those who have fled to the mountains so bare look down

on the victims with loving despair

If only they'd known enough to flee and stand on the stark hill

of Calvary

They would have found no price to high

For the sweet air of Freedom and the clear blue sky
Yes, the mantle of God, is blue and serene
And gives us the freedom we crave
And the word of God is life and love beyond this earth and the
grave
And stark, tho the Hill of Calvary
May appear with cross so plain
Those who flee to the arms of God
Will find warmth and release from pain
So heed not the Evil mantle of Red
But cling to the Mantle of Blue instead
Have faith – have hope, and if you must
Defend these things in which we trust
And pray that we might someday release
From the iron grip of Red
All that long for freedom and God's mantle overhead

<u>REMEMBER GOD</u>

Remember my children in the long dark night
When you reach out in loneliness or fear
That with the dawn comes a lovely light
And until the dawn – God is near
Don't hate Him for things you don't understand,
Or blame Him because you feel lost
For He knows how you feel – remember for you – He too bore a
heavy cross
And if you should lose someone you love
And bitterness grows within

Think now! Don't you hope – With all your heart –
That your loved one dwells with Him?
And until the day we go to Him
We have life abundantly
He gave me all of you my dears
And His gift to you - was me.
And I love you so, I've held you near
Watched as you laughed and cried
And the memories we all hold dear can never – ever die
Could He give us all so much and still be cruel and mean?
That's like saying someone's fat and at the same time lean!
Follow His commandments – be kind to one another
For every soul within this world is your sister or your brother
Change the faults within yourselves
Don't point them out in those you meet
Or someday you may walk within their shoes
Down dark and lonely streets
Remember – God is watching
As ye judge so you'll be judged
And the only way to win a heart is love
My children – Love!

THE SACRIFICE

The night has gone
Yet day is not yet here
The world is hushed
Its dawn
Soft mist and light diffuses the darkness
Beginning another day
A time of solitude

To think – remember – pray
Yet knowing
Accepting this beginning might
Bring harsh reality
As He did know
So long ago
In the garden of Gethsemane
That He begged the bitter cup
He would not have to taste
Yet drank the full of it
The anger of the multitude
Laid His body waste
Then spit upon Him in their anger
Thinking they had won
When at last they heard Him say
"Father it is done!"
Save yourself – they jeered Him
He can't – He's just a man
They'd done their worst
But His spirit lived
Christianity began
So if you are called a dreamer, a fool
Condemned as useless and weak
So _even_ was the Son of God
As He turned the other cheek
A waiting time
Then He rose again
In the hush of another dawn
A promise
He would someday return
Then quietly was gone!
He knows how you feel
He felt it too
Hurt, despair and pain
But He conquered all
And so can you
Thru His Holy Name!

SIREN'S SONG

There's a story--very old,
A mystic story often told,
By Mariners at sea--
That when the moon is low and full--Beware!
Lest then--you feel the pull
Of Altered Destiny!
'Tis on such nights--
That--like a child
Grown men--"are lulled"
And then beguiled
By the Siren's Song
Sweet and sad in content and a lifetime long
Knowing of the dangers
Wise sailors block their ears
Overcome temptation to listen to the "Song of Tears"
So beautiful--compelling
It weaves a tragic spell
To catch the heart--
Bind the will
Then lead the soul "To Hell!"
So too the song that you once sang
A haunting melody
That spoke of how my love for you
Would heal and set you free
Of loneliness and doubt
That filled your childhood years
My heart was caught
That moment in your veil of tears
And soon my will was bound
As it became your own
The cloak of sadness was for me, the heaviest I have known
Still, never did my love for you, break the tragic spell
But only led, in time, my soul-- to the Gates of Hell
Then came My Lord to rescue me
From the Siren Song
Sweet an sad in content
But a lifetime long!

I wonder how it would have been
If I had blocked my ears
Overcome temptation to listen--to "The Song of Tears"
But tho I wonder--it's too late
My youth--my life--is gone!
All because I listened--to the Siren's Song.

STRENGTH

Heed the breaking of my heart
As this shattered spirit falls
Weep with my soul -- in heaven's realm
Lord of beauty -- Lord of love,
Truth and loyalty --
Have pity on your daughter --
Come abide with me --
Impart to me your courage
That I may live, within this hell
As you would have me live, even tho I dwell --
Underneath the shadow of great unholy wings
Surrounded by the agony his very shadow brings
But greater than the evil one "The Holy Trinity"
Penetrate this darkness -- shed your light on me
Let me rest within the strength -- that rolled away the stone
Let Easter come, that I may <u>know</u> -- I am not alone!
Lead to me then to Zion -- protect me with your staff
From the hounds of hell -- their fury and their wrath
For they have long tormented me --
Each time I tried to follow thee --
Forbid them, now, I pray --

Faced with the blood of holy love
They must turn away

TAKE MY HAND

Jesus take me gently by the hand
Lead me thru this strange and hostile land
Fold your cloak around me when I'm cold
Where there is fear and danger make me bold
Sing to me when I am weary Lord
Shield me from the enemy's sharp sword
Jesus take me gently by the hand
Guide me to your Father's holy land

THEIR LOVE

I would tell the World this day
Of the many strange, and Wondrous ways -
My God has seen me thru -
This vale of Tears called Planet Earth -
The dwelling place, that since my birth
I have been one of you!
No easy place in which to live -
To love - to hope - keep faith - and give
This place where death abounds -
It can't be done - where there's just one-
Unless, perhaps - you've found -
The secret - that's no secret -

A Gift from God above
Proclaimed by Jesus - Son of God -
"Pure, Unselfish Love"!
The only thing with power to unlock the gates of hell -
Or sooth the wounds inflicted by this world On which we
dwell -
And even when you feel - a sad and lonely "one"
Lean on his love - and you will find -
"Your life has just begun!"
For he'll reveal - Horizons you never dreamed were there -
Bring his people to surround you - to show you that they care
His love will strengthen, aid you, to bear the heavy cross,
Open ways to show you - you are saved -
You are not lost.
So keep your eyes upon the light
If you should go astray -
Then he will guide you lovingly -
Along the Father's Way,
The Holy Spirit will Insure that even, should you fall -
You can rise, to try once more - and finally Conquer all!
Love is all - you have to give -
Returning then - to help you live -
As He would have you do!
He said "faithful unto me - I shall faithful unto you"!
So if your life seems hopeless - reach out - do not despair!
For even in the darkness - He loves you, He is there!
Perhaps you need to feel the fright, the loss, the pain of Sin -
To need once more the Holy light that leads you back to Him!

He always knows if you rebel - then leaves you feeling all
alone
Waiting for your call once more -
So he can lead you home!
For rest assured, he, in love, will do what he must do,
Tho sometimes it must wound his heart,
To turn away from you -
He will - Until you realize - your desperate need of him,
Kneel and ask forgiveness - Repent of all your sins -
- Tis then the "Lamb of God" will wash them all away -
With "His Blood" - Shed just for you
That Crucifixion Day -
You'll never be the same again -
Nor Will you wish to be !
I know ! For I was on my knees -
When Jesus - Lovingly -
Sent his Holy Spirit - With Grace from God above,
Saving me ! This Trinity ! With the
Power of - - "Their Love !"

THY WILL

Come show a blinding light that will dispel all darkness
Fill the corners of the Earth show all the ugly things for what
they're worth
Root out the crawlers of the night
No more evil little thoughts in minds that pose as pure
No thieves, molesters, crucifiers-child beaters, drunks,
murderers or liars

Working their plans in dark and ugly places
For light so bright that it will show debauchery on their very
faces
And they will try to crawl into their nests and throw
themselves
in terror against a solid wall
Nowhere to hide, their evil all revealed
Their names called out for everyone to hear
Their sentence levied not to be repealed.
Their voices blaming all but themselves.
Turning on each other in their fear
Then only will the earth be cleansed
A prophecy fulfilled-
Come show a blinding light we need it so
Carry out your promise of long ago
Enforce your Holy Will!

THE AGONY

Jesus Christ! I call on you – in agony and pain
In anger at injustice – I call your holy name
See the people dying – hear the people pray
See the children crying, as darkness fills their day
See the soldiers marching thru the stricken land
The proud destroyers, following their leader's cruel commands
Negotiating peace – tho war is their desire
Souls aflame with hatred, minds aflame with fire
Bestial creatures, killing all who would disagree
Filled with self importance, they do not look to see
The toll they take of those who live – for love – for peace – for
Thee!
And so it is, as it has been, thru the ages past

The Lamb is carried to His death
Upon the stubborn ass
They close their ears to cries of pain
It matters not to them
They war, and kill, destroy, and maim
It is the way of men
<u>*Who do not care what God has said,*</u>
<u>*That Christ was crucified*</u>
All these things they know, yet they still defy
The written law of God's own will
As to God – they cry
Give us victory – we are right!
We shall prove it thru our might1
Dear Lord strike the Bloody sword
From their senseless hand
Bring sanity and justice
To our Stricken land
Drive the foe, far below, shackle him in chains!
We need you Lord, please help us!
Come dwell with us again!
Deliver us from Evil – Let Thy will be done
That all the children of this earth
Led by Your wondrous Son
May dwell once more in peace and love
Their land once more renewed
Their lives restored to sanity
Thru love, thru grace, thru You!
Amen

THE TREASURE

"The pain" – so great the pain ---
Don't know what to do ---
"Once" I did! "Now" I don't!
The pain --- The pain --- "IS YOU!"
You came into my life

You touched my very soul
With love and dreams and wondrous things
And then I watched you go.
Nothing I could do – Nothing I could say
As one by one, each wondrous gift, you broke or gave away!
Until the place was empty – That once you used to fill
My love for you could not compete against your "anger" or
your "will"
I tried to mend the broken pieces – put them together, once again
But edges of a shattered dream are sharp – and filled with pain
And those who dare to touch them
Shall be filled with agony – for
"In the pieces" – are reflected
"All that used to be"
And tho "I know" – "from pieces"
"I cannot build Anew"
My soul, "cannot" – somehow, "discard!"
These remnants, left by you!
"So tho" they have no value – except to God – To me
I'll take, these treasured pieces,
Into Eternity!
Perhaps – When God receives them
"He'll" – know – "what to do"-
With "little pieces" – of the "Love"
"I once" – "received" – "from you" –
"For"- "He too" – "was broken" –
Upon Golgotha's Hill
"In agony" – "for love of us" "Gave Body, Soul and Will"
To form a bridge – that we might know
Where Love – In bits and pieces – Go!

UNIVERSAL GIFTS

I wish, I could, in words convey --
How much you mean to me each day
How every smile, every touch, is like a priceless treasure
Held within the heart and soul --
"There" -- to live forever
If from Heaven's Warehouse, I'd chosen those I'd love
I couldn't, in a million years - I swear by God above –
Chosen better --For all of you were perfect, Loves , for Me
Was that a chuckle I just heard? You don't quite agree?
Ah, then you're remembering --when you'd thought you should
be better-
Followed others' protocol -- Strictly to the letter
All your imagined faults, gave you identity!
Mom and Dad, Brother, Sister, Children, Husband, Friends,
All of you -- acquaintances, In this world, there is no end
For some have gone, But I meet new ones every single day-
Sure as God made sour apples - More are on the way
Grandchildren and their assorted friends --
The little boy that smiled,
The would-be artist who looked at paints and brushes
Totally Beguiled --
When I stop to really think of what God's done for me --
I feel a love that overflows
Into eternity --
And touches all creation -- brings me to my knees
In humble adoration, in pure ecstasy --
For you and all His gifts My Loves
Because he values me

Imagine!
Me!
Shirley Ann Wood!
Wow!

VOICE OF GOD

God speaks to many
In many tongues
But one language --
End of all commands
Entreats, repeats
The most important one
Care for me
For each other, and
Care for all the land
Of all you'll know
Or read or learn
You are children still
Do not destroy but
Love and build
This is my holy will
My loved protects surrounds
You like the fluid of
Your mother's womb
And suffered greatly
For you to raise you
From year tomb
Take heed or you'll destroy

Each other and your dwelling place
Then his anger shall be heard
Thu eons and thru space
The various spheres shall tremble
The sun shall hide it's light
Then man shall know
What he has known
In the terror of the night
That he is not a power
He imagined he might be
But subject to the power
Of he who created all
The one the true,
The living God of all eternity

WALK WITH GOD

I walk in the shadow of no man
When I walk in the light of God
For in His light I see things clearly
It dispels all doubt and fear
With head held High I walk with surety
Toward a goal which now seems near
For I am His daughter and I am unique
Unlike any other
And I am one with Him
With you — my sister and my brother
For each of you are loved by Him
The very same as I

He hears each prayer – knows your doubts
Hears each lonely sigh
Some will disappoint Him
And for these He'll leave His flock
To search for them and comfort them, hoping to unlock
Their hearts – their minds
That He might save them
From Pitfalls in the night
He loves you! – listen to Him!
Walk within His light
For in this light is understanding
In understanding there is love
Therein lies mans' freedom
Don't you see? It's clear!
Real Happiness – real freedom
Is the total lack of "fear"
For without fear there's no avarice
No jealousy or hate
And therefore there's no danger
But the hour now grows late
Don't wait! Do away with Fright
You'll walk in no man's Shadow
When you walk in our Father's Light!

THE WAY OF LOVE

I Am Of "Him" - Jesus Said, The Truth, The Light, The Way
I Give You Life - Tho You Be Dead -
May Love "Alone" Can Saey -

The Heavenly Father From His Wrath
When You Choose The Darkened Path -
So Turn Now - Follow Me!
Trust In "The Word" It's Power"-
To Set All Peoples Free!
Why Does The World - Refuse To Heed-
Our Saviour's Counsel - Still?
Devastating Lives And Lands With Their Unholy Will?
Why Do We Judge Our Brethren,
Yet Never Look Within -
To Find The Truth, The Light, The Way -
From Hate - From War - From Sin?
All - Who Worship - Death And Sin -
"Beguile " - - With Words - - Untrue,
Thru The Lusts Of Earthly Flesh -
They Seek - The Soul - Of You
Your "Gift Of Life", Your "Gift Of Love -
"From God!" To - One And All-
Thru His Power It Shall Rise!
With ought Him - It - Shall Fall!
"Believe In Him", And Do Not Fear -
When It Is Time To Die -
For Thru His Love - And By His Blood -
Death He Did Defy! - - - And Conquered -
For He Lives! And Has Prepared A Place -
Wondrous To Behold - Filled With His Gentle Grace!
Bask In The Wondrous Glory -
His Presence Does Impart -
Receive "Life" - "Everlasting" - From - "Loves" -
Eternal Heart!

YOU CHOOSE

I love my God with all my heart,
And on the day I must depart
I shall go to be with him
For, His Son, Lord Jesus –
Has washed away my sins
Some folks say – How <u>can</u> you know?
They don't believe such things are so
They don't seem to understand, why I do – How I can!
For I've been hurt, so many times
Enough to break this heart of mine
They think I should be bitter – and blame
Others for my pain –
But God has spoken to my heart
Time and time again –
"I LOVE YOU" - you are lucky – for thru
Your pain you've learned
That envy, malice, unforgiveness,
Causes souls to burn
With dissatisfaction – they search both night and day
To gather earthly treasures, wandering far away
From the greatest treasure in heaven or on earth
The gift of love to one another
Depicted by the birth
Of My Son – Who brought to you
This message sent by Me – wrapped in love